PROWLING the SEAS

Exploring the Hidden World of Ocean Predators

PROWLING
the SEAS

Exploring the Hidden World of Ocean Predators

Pamela S. Turner

WALKER & COMPANY

New York

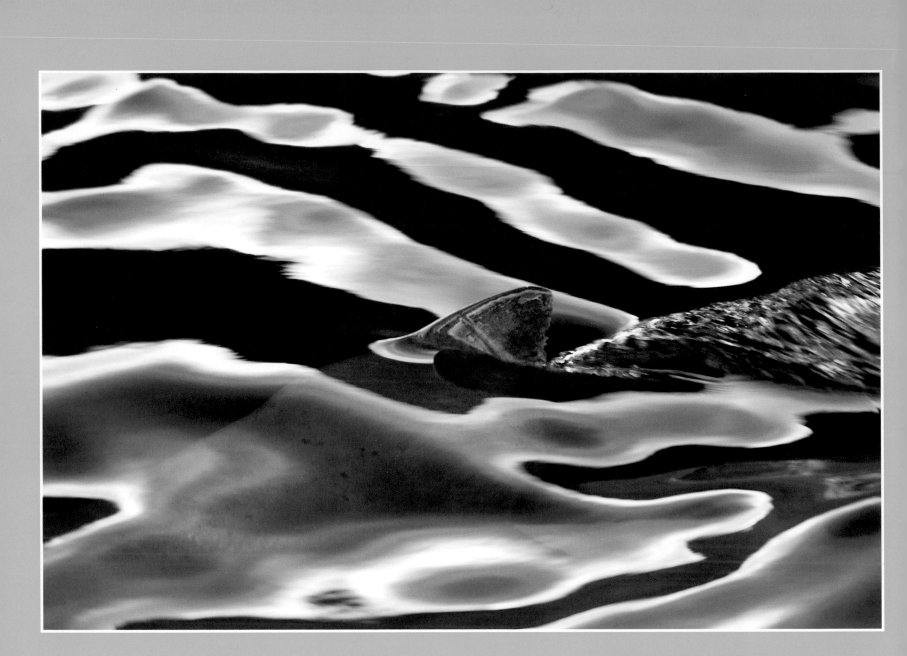

The tip of a white shark's fin. (The species is known as the "great white shark," but scientists call them "white sharks.")

INTRODUCTION
The Other Side of the Sea

The bluefin tuna are hunting. They speed through the water toward a school of baitfish. The baitfish scatter, but many do not escape.

A leatherback sea turtle glides below the bluefin. As she flaps her long front flippers, she looks like a bird flying in slow motion. High above, lost in the clouds, a seabird flies on silent wings.

A great white shark swims nearby. Her coal-black eyes roll toward the surface. She is looking for a seal. If a seal passes above her, she will see its dark form against the sunlit surface. She will ambush it from below.

A long, dark shape passes steadily overhead—the hull of a boat. The white shark feels and hears the thrumming of engines. She swims on.

From the boat, you can't spot the tuna below or the seabird high above. You can't know the sea turtle's grace. Your heart doesn't thump, because the white shark is hidden. You see only storm-gray water stretching endlessly in every direction. You might think: "The open ocean is as lifeless as the moon."

CLOCKWISE FROM TOP LEFT:
Yellowfin tuna,
sperm whale,
salmon shark,
Humboldt squid,
Laysan albatross,
loggerhead sea turtle,
juvenile elephant seal,
sooty shearwater,
California sea lion,
ocean sunfish

Tagging Pacific Predators

When we think of predators, we often think of lions, bears, and tigers. Yet most of the world's predators don't live on land. They live in the sea.

Scientists have long wanted to know more about ocean predators such as sharks, tuna, seabirds, and sea turtles. Where do they breed? How do they find food? Where do they travel? How do the things we humans do, such as fishing, affect them?

It is difficult to study the sea and the animals that live there. Scientists can pull ocean animals out of the water with scoops and nets, but many ocean animals cannot survive in glass tanks. Scientists can go out in boats or dive with scuba gear, but ocean animals can easily swim away.

There is one thing scientists *do* know about ocean wildlife. Surveys and fishing data show that the numbers of many ocean animals have declined rapidly. More than 90 percent of all large fish, such as sharks, swordfish, and bluefin tuna, are gone. Too many have been caught by fishermen.

Other ocean predators are also at risk. Many seabirds drown because they grab baited hooks as fishermen throw the hooks into the water. Sea turtles swallow hooks too. Sea turtles can also drown in fishing nets because they must come to the surface to breathe.

"These animals are disappearing from the world's oceans," says Dr. Barbara (Barb) Block of Stanford University. "We are trying to understand open-ocean predators and save them."

Barb and other scientists are part of the Tagging of Pacific Predators (TOPP) project. TOPP scientists use high-tech tags to collect data from whales, fish, seals, sea lions, sharks, sea turtles, seabirds, and large squid as they journey across the open ocean. Through their tags, these animals give us a glimpse into their vast blue world.

CHAPTER ONE
The Great Turtle Race

A lime-green moon shines overhead as Genevieve lumbers up the beach. The leatherback sea turtle is searching for the perfect sand: not too dry, not too wet. When she finds it, she uses her back flippers to dig a hole and begins laying eggs.

George Shillinger and his team tiptoe up to Genevieve. For twenty minutes or so, while the turtle is laying eggs, she goes into a trance. She is calm and will allow people around her. George and his team dig a tunnel under Genevieve's belly and strap on her harness.

The eggs look like Ping-Pong balls as they plop into the nest. Genevieve snorts and grunts. Saltwater drips from her eyes. This is how sea turtles rid their bodies of salt, but it looks like Genevieve is crying.

Her satellite tag, strapped to her harness, is ready to go. So is Genevieve. She buries her eggs with gentle swipes of her back flippers. Next, she turns in circles, flinging sand in all directions. Her nest is now hidden. At last, Genevieve drags her immense body back to the water. She's the first to enter the Great Turtle Race!

A tagged leatherback slips back into the ocean. Her harness carries a satellite tag. When the sea turtle comes to the surface to breathe, the tag sends its data to satellites orbiting high above Earth. The satellites then send the data to the scientists' computers.

A female leatherback sheds salty tears. Female leatherbacks nest at night, when there are fewer predators around. Each female will nest about seven times and lay about 100 eggs in each nest.

From previous years' data, George knows that most of the turtles nesting on the Playa Grande in Costa Rica will swim to the Galápagos Islands when they've finished laying eggs. So why not have a "race"? It will raise money for research and teach people about sea turtles. "Racing turtles—it just sounds so funny!" says George.

Eleven schools and businesses donate money to name "their" turtle. In April 2007 Genevieve, Billie, Champiro, Drexelina, Freedom, Purple Lightning, Saphira, Stephanie Colburtle, Sundae, Turtleocity, and Windy are on their way to the Galápagos, 750 miles (1,200 kilometers) west. The Great Turtle Race is on!

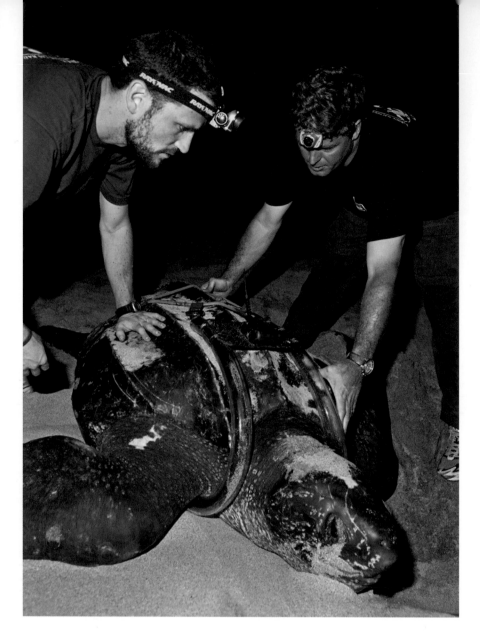

A leatherback's harness is designed to fall off in about eighteen months. Leatherbacks can grow to be 6.5 feet (2 meters) long, and they can weigh up to 2,000 pounds (900 kilograms). No one knows exactly how long they live, but some of the females at Playa Grande are at least thirty years old.

The turtles' tags send data to a satellite orbiting Earth. The satellite, in turn, sends the data to TOPP scientists. The scientists post a map on a Web site that shows where the turtles are. The Web site explains that the leatherbacks head toward the Galápagos after nesting because the waters around the islands are full of jellyfish—the leatherback's favorite food.

Swimming to the Galápagos can be dangerous. The turtles must battle strong currents. They must escape their natural predators: tiger sharks and killer whales. Unfortunately, humans create the most hazards. Baited hooks and fishing nets can snare turtles. Sometimes turtles die from eating plastic bags. Floating plastic bags look like floating jellyfish.

Thousands of people visit the race's Web site to cheer on their favorite turtle. The students at Bullis Charter School in Los Altos, California, are especially excited. They are sponsoring Saphira in the Great Turtle Race.

On the third day of the race, Windy is out in front. Billie is second. While tagging Billie, George noticed she has notches in both rear flippers. He thinks she may have been nipped by predators when she was small. Drexelina and Sundae are still swimming near Playa Grande.

By day seven, tension is mounting. Stephanie, the biggest turtle in the race, takes the lead. Billie veers north but stays in second place. Purple Lightning wanders south. So does Turtleocity, one of the smallest turtles in the race. On day nine, Billie's route north seems to be paying off. She surges ahead of Stephanie. Has Billie caught a swift current, or is she a speed demon?

On day eleven, Billie swims gracefully over an invisible finish line. She wins! Stephanie finishes second on day twelve. A few hours later, Champiro noses out Turtleocity for third. Purple Lightning, Genevieve, and Saphira cross the finish line on day thirteen. By day fourteen, Freedom and Windy arrive in the Galápagos.

Drexelina and Sundae? Those pokey turtles are still swimming off Costa Rica.

Baby turtles hatch on Playa Grande, which is the last major leatherback nesting beach on the Pacific coast of the Americas.

Baby leatherback turtles begin their own race for survival. The females, if they live to become adults, will return to Playa Grande to lay their eggs.

The Great Turtle Race brings in more than $200,000 for turtle research. And thousands of Web site visitors learn that leatherbacks are in a race against extinction. In 1990 about 1,000 leatherback sea turtles nested at Playa Grande. Now only about 100 arrive to lay their eggs.

Two months after the Great Turtle Race, there is a baby race on the beach. The eggs hatch. Baby turtles struggle out of their nests. They are hardly bigger than the palm of a man's hand, but they are strong. They must be quick to avoid being eaten by predators such as seabirds. Each little turtle dashes for the safety of the sea.

And the mothers? The tags on some of the racing turtles keep working. Ten months after the Great Turtle Race, George declares Genevieve the winner of the "Super Swimathon." She's flapped her flippers 4,770 miles (7,680 kilometers) since nesting.

After all, Genevieve's a turtle. Slow and steady wins the race!

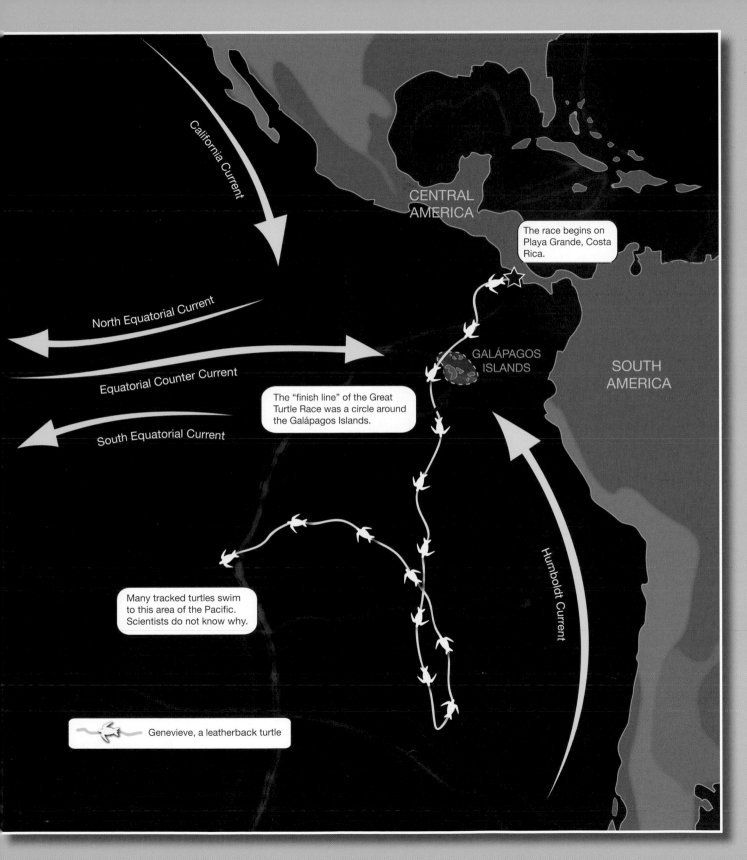

The race begins on Playa Grande, Costa Rica.

California Current

CENTRAL AMERICA

North Equatorial Current

Equatorial Counter Current

South Equatorial Current

GALÁPAGOS ISLANDS

SOUTH AMERICA

The "finish line" of the Great Turtle Race was a circle around the Galápagos Islands.

Humboldt Current

Many tracked turtles swim to this area of the Pacific. Scientists do not know why.

Genevieve, a leatherback turtle

Knowing where the turtles go is important. Scientists can use the tagging data to help fishermen avoid catching the turtles by accident in their nets.

13

CHAPTER TWO
The Little Tuna That Could

The young bluefin tuna swims on and on, never stopping. Water passing into its mouth and through its gills gives it oxygen for breathing. The water also carries tastes and smells. To us, taste and smell are different senses, but not to a fish.

Overhead, the *thrum . . . thrum . . .* of a boat engine sends tiny ripples of sound through the water. The tuna senses the tiny sound waves as they touch the tuna's body. To us, feeling and hearing are different senses, but not to a fish.

Food! Does the young tuna feel/hear the sardine wiggling on the hook? Or smell/taste sardine-scented water? Or see the sardine's shape against the sparkling surface? Maybe all three. The young tuna is always hungry. The tuna snatches the sardine—and finds itself pulled aboard a fishing boat.

Barb Block inserted a high-tech tag in this bluefin tuna. A sensor sticks out of its body to read the water temperature and track its location. Another sensor inside the tuna's body senses the depth of the water the tuna swims in and the temperature of the fish's body.

Like mammals (but unlike most other fish) bluefin tuna are warm-blooded. Warm blood, a large heart, and powerful swimming muscles help bluefin catch fast-moving prey.

Barb Block lays the tuna in a plastic sling. She puts a wet towel over the young tuna's eyes to keep it calm. The young bluefin is slightly less than 3 feet (1 meter) long and weighs 33 pounds (15 kilograms). Barb doesn't know if the tuna is male or female, because both sexes look the same on the outside. But from the tuna's size, she guesses it is about two and a half years old.

Within minutes the tuna has its tag. Barb and her team slip the tuna back into the ocean. It darts away with a few powerful thrusts of its tail.

For the next seven months, the young tuna stays in the food-rich waters of the California Current. It probably joins schools of other young bluefin. The lightning-quick tuna are like tornados with teeth as they attack schools of anchovies, sardines, squid, and red crabs.

In spring 2003 the young tuna turns west and swims steadily for almost two months. Barb calls the tuna's route "the highway across the Pacific" because so many other tagged tuna travel along this same path. The young bluefin swims to an area off Japan. It finds seamounts (underwater mountains) that attract many small fish and squid—and, of course, many predators. As the tuna eats, it must also keep an eye out for animals that would like to eat *it*: killer whales, dolphins, and sharks.

In midsummer, the tuna follows the "ocean highway" east. By August it is hunting again in the California Current. The tuna stays six months. Then—once again—the bluefin crosses the Pacific to feed near the seamounts.

On June 7, 2004, the tuna's epic swim comes to an end. It is caught in a net by a Japanese fisherman. He returns the tag. Barb and her student Andre Boustany are very surprised when they download the fish's data into their computers.

Chuck Farwell of the Monterey Bay Aquarium covers a young bluefin's eyes to keep it calm.

Tuna have been called "the perfect fish" because their bodies move through the water so easily. Engineers study tuna in order to design better submarines.

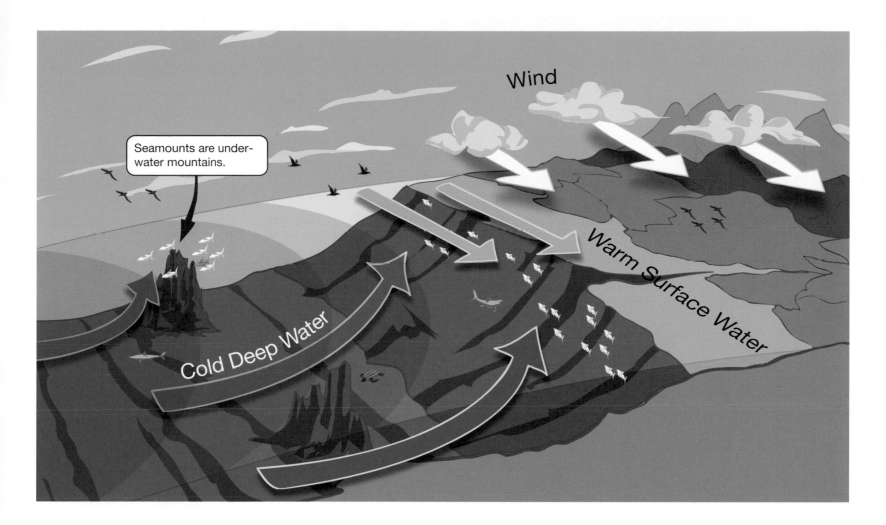

Coastal currents are like rivers within the ocean. As wind pushes the top (warmer) layer of ocean water, cold water is pulled from the depths and curls up against the coastline. This cold water has nutrients (energy-rich chemicals) that help plankton (tiny floating plants and animals) grow. Small fish, crabs, and jellyfish eat plankton, and are in turn fed on by larger predators.

Barb and Andre know that northern Pacific bluefin hatch in the warm waters off Japan, and some young bluefin make a trip to California and Mexico. But they thought that bluefin cross the Pacific twice, at most, during their lifetime. This young tuna crossed the Pacific *three* times in less than 600 days—a 25,000-mile (40,230-kilometer) journey. That's farther than the distance around our entire planet! And since Pacific bluefin are spawned (born from eggs laid in the water) near Japan, the young fish must have crossed the Pacific *four* times during its short life.

Bluefin tuna caught in a net. Most people think of tuna as sandwich filling, but bluefin tuna are one of the ocean's great predators.

Bluefin tuna for sale in Japan. In 2001 a single bluefin sold here for $175,000. You won't find bluefin tuna in fish sticks, sandwiches, or tacos. It is luxury food for the wealthy.

Barb was glad to get the data. Yet it worries her that half of her tagged bluefin are caught by fishermen. Most are caught before they are old enough to mate. That is why there are so few left.

"There is a worldwide hunt for bluefin tuna," says Barb. "Most people don't know about it, but it is happening every day in every ocean. It is the last 'gold rush' on Earth."

The young bluefin tuna was a real survivor. It found its way back and forth across a vast ocean, always hunting, always swimming. But it didn't survive the human appetite for bluefin.

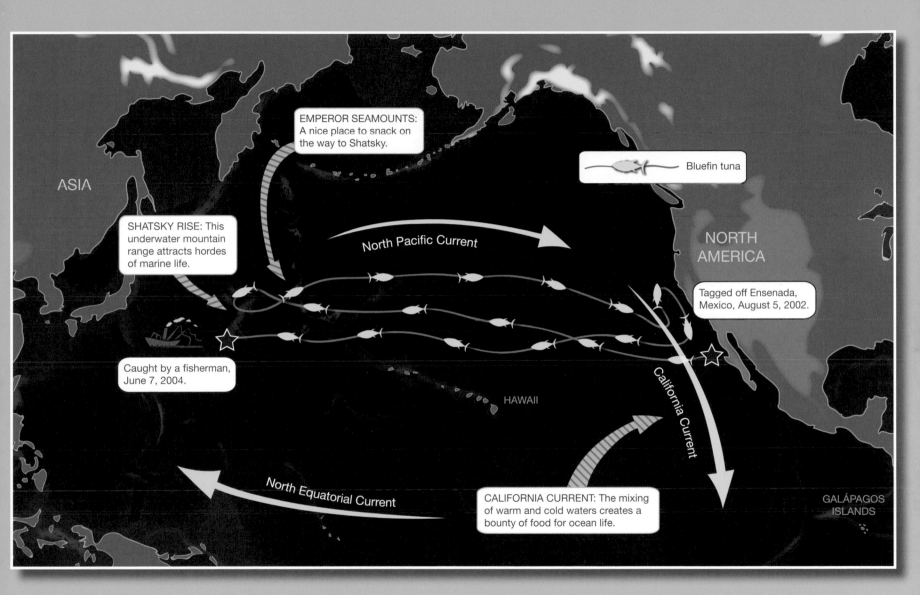

The little tuna swam an average of 40 miles (64 kilometers) every day. Scientists wonder how tuna find their way across the ocean. Do they get clues from the sun? From the taste/smell of the water? Earth itself is like a very weak magnet—can the fish sense tiny magnetic differences from place to place and use them as signposts? No one knows.

CHAPTER THREE
White Shark Mystery

Five-year-old Calvin with the white shark tag he discovered in a tide pool at Sea Ranch, California.

On the day after Christmas 2005, five-year-old Calvin Wisner was exploring tide pools with his parents. He found soft, squishy sea anemones and watched crabs scramble sideways over the rocks.

His sharp eyes caught a glimmer of metal among the rocks. It looked like a microphone—but a microphone doesn't have a wire sticking out of the top.

Calvin and his parents carried the gadget back to their family's vacation house. No one knew what it was. But a name was printed on the side: *Wildlife Computers*.

Calvin's grandfather called the company. He learned that Calvin had found a high-tech TOPP tag full of important scientific data. When Calvin returns the tag to the scientists, he will get a $500 reward. "Cool!" said Calvin.

Best of all, Calvin discovered that his tag belonged to one of the sea's greatest predators: a great white shark.

About a year earlier, shark scientist Scot Anderson was sitting in his 17-foot (5-meter) boat, the *Porpoise*, off Tomales Point in Northern California. Swirling water told him something big was swimming just below the surface. Scot worked quickly to put a dart on the end of a 6-foot (2-meter) metal pole. A high-tech tag was attached to the dart by a short plastic line.

The shark swam past the boat. But Scot's pole wasn't ready. Scot wondered if he would get a second chance.

Once again, the dark shape glided near. Scot jabbed the dart tip into the muscle just behind the shark's fin. He filmed the shark with his pole-mounted video camera as it swam away. It was a 13-foot- (4-meter-) long female. She was not quite an adult—but

A female white shark on patrol. Females grow bigger than males. Females as large as 19 feet (6 meters) have been seen off California.

this teenager weighed about 1,500 pounds (680 kilograms)!

The white shark stayed along the Northern California coast for another six weeks. She may have caught a nice fat seal or two. But by mid-February most of the seals and sea lions were leaving to hunt fish in the open ocean. The white shark left too.

The shark traveled far into the Pacific Ocean. Most of the time she swam just below the sunlit surface. Sometimes she dived more than 2,000 feet (610 meters) down. Like the bluefin tuna, the white shark was always tasting/smelling the water and feeling/hearing for the ripples made by prey swimming nearby. Did the shark find fish to eat in those dark, cold waters?

White sharks will often come near Scot's boat. Scot works from small boats because larger boats frighten the sharks.

After five weeks, the white shark reached Hawaii. Perhaps she found Hawaii's surface waters too warm, because now she spent most of her time in the cool depths between 100 and 1,600 feet (30 and 490 meters). She was probably hunting tuna, spinner dolphins, and monk seals. At the end of April the shark swam to a spot south of Hawaii.

The white shark's "pop-up" satellite tag was set to release in mid-July. It was supposed to pop off the shark, float to the surface, and send its data to an orbiting satellite. The satellite was supposed to send the shark's data to the

As a curious white shark passes his boat, Scot sticks a pole-mounted video camera into the water to film it. Using the camera, he can identify individual sharks by the nicks and scars on their bodies. He also uses the camera to tell if a shark is male or female.

Scot can recognize many sharks by the scars and nicks on their bodies. TOPP scientists have nicknames for some of the sharks they study. Tipfin, Carl Ripfin, Bitehead, and Stumpy are among the sharks Scot has known.

TOPP scientists. But on June 12, 2005, the tag's battery died. The tag never popped up. Six months later, Calvin found it floating in a Northern California tide pool. How did the tag get from Hawaii to California?

Scot Anderson thinks the young white shark carried the tag back to California. Data from other tagged sharks show that white sharks travel from California to Hawaii and back again. But how did the tag come off the shark?

The only clue: long, deep scratches on the shark's tag. Teeth marks.

A sea lion follows a white shark. This is probably NOT a good idea.

Scot with his video camera at Northern California's Farallon Islands. This camera was later knocked out of his hands by a white shark's powerful tail.

It might have been another white shark. Among many kinds of sharks, males and females snap at each other during mating. Was it a love bite?

Some fish, like ling cod, are very aggressive. Did one mistake the tag for a small silver fish? "Ling cod will bite almost anything flashy," says Scot.

There is another possibility. Although white sharks eat seals and sea lions, seals and sea lions are faster swimmers. They will sometimes swim up behind a white shark and nip at it. It's like a squirrel teasing a dog, or a crow attacking a hawk. Did a snappy seal or sea lion bite off the white shark's tag?

Scot thinks it's all a minor miracle. "To get this shark's data took so much effort at so many levels," he says. "The people who designed the tag, the work of the research team, the shark dragging the tag around, and Calvin finding the tag and returning it to us."

And as Calvin says: "The whole thing is pretty cool."

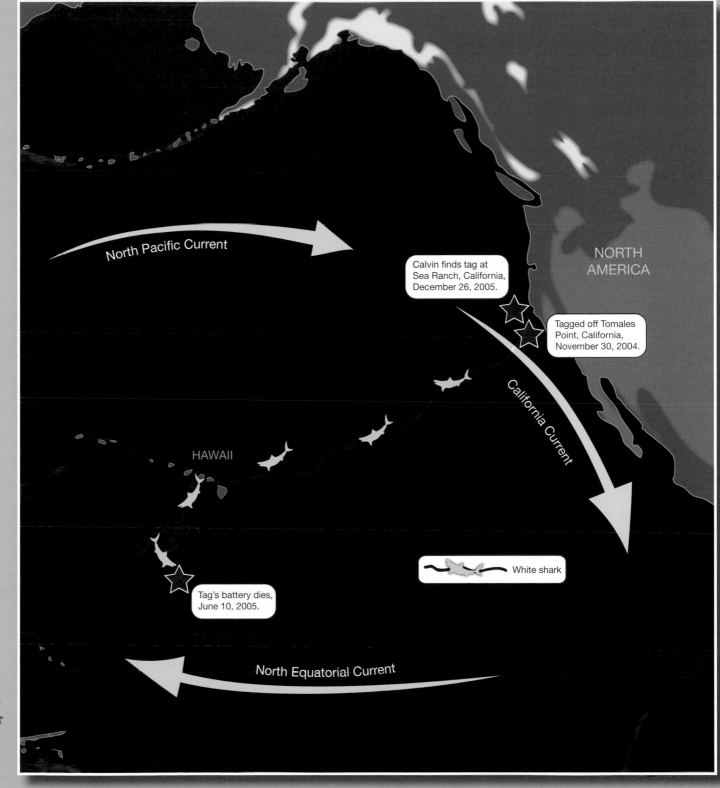

The young female white shark traveled from California to Hawaii. Scientists once thought white sharks stayed near the coast. But TOPP's high-tech tags have shown that white sharks travel far into the open ocean.

Scott Shaffer reaches into a shearwater burrow for a fluffy chick. Shearwaters nest in holes in the ground, which they return to every year. "The trick is to find a burrow with only one entrance," says Scott.

CHAPTER FOUR
Seabird Safari

The moaning goes on all night long. It floats out of the darkness, through the trees and ferns. Codfish Island, New Zealand, sounds like it is full of ghosts. But the island is really full of seabirds.

Scott Shaffer checks burrow #B111. Both parents are huddled inside next to their chick. Scott pulls out the female sooty shearwater. She looks indignant as Scott and his helpers strap a tag on her leg. Her mate gets one too.

At dawn the male and female scramble out of their burrow. They beat their wings as if happy to greet the sun. They call—a throaty *whhoo-whhoo*. So do thousands of other birds. The whole forest hums with seabird song.

Sooty shearwaters are found all around the Pacific. Scott thinks the birds travel in a huge circle around

The researchers often work at night, when mated seabirds return to their burrows. But sometimes the curious shearwaters decide to study the scientists.

the rim of the ocean. But over the next nine months the seabirds' tags will tell a different story.

The pair of sooty shearwaters from Burrow #B111 stays near Codfish Island for another four weeks. On March 3, 2005, the male leaves. Twelve days later the female leaves too. Their chick must now fend for itself.

Both tagged birds catch the "westerlies"—winds blowing steadily from west to east. FLAP-FLAP-FLAP-*g l i d e*. FLAP-FLAP-FLAP-*g l i d e*. By the end of March the shearwaters reach the coast of South America. Just as the California Current mixes warm and cold waters off North America, the Humboldt Current mixes warm and cold waters off South America. These rich waters attract many fish and squid.

How do the shearwaters find their way to this feeding ground? How do they spot food under the rippling water?

Seabirds probably use the sun and moon as guides. Sooty shearwaters also have a good sense of smell. The Humboldt Current is near South America, so the earthy smell of land may be a clue. And scientists think some seabirds can smell thick mats of floating plankton. Fish feeding on the plankton are in turn eaten by seabirds and other predators.

Shearwaters find food with their sharp eyes too. The seabirds watch for whales circling a school of krill (a kind of shrimp), or baitfish leaping up out of the water to escape the jaws of bluefin tuna. The male and female shearwaters dive into the water to capture their prey.

A flock of sooty shearwaters gathers off Northern California.

The female seems to like the buffet along the Humboldt Current. She spends a month, but her mate stays only a week. He flies away on trade winds blowing northwest. Food can be scarce in the warm waters around the equator, so the shearwater flies fast and straight. The sun warms his back and the cool wind lifts his belly. FLAP-FLAP-FLAP-*g l i d e*. FLAP-FLAP-FLAP-*g l i d e*. Sometimes the seabird rests on the water.

A few weeks later, the male reaches the coast of Japan. He is probably very hungry. But he has found a place where two currents, one warmer and one cooler, flow past each other. The swirling ocean is fish-rich.

His mate does not join him. Instead, she flies northwest. The female shearwater passes just south of the Galápagos Islands, where leatherback sea turtles like to feed on jellyfish. The female makes a big loop and then turns toward the west coast of the United States. She arrives in Oregon at the end of April. For the next five months the female shearwater goes up and down the coasts of Oregon, California, and Mexico. She eats at the California Current cafeteria along with many other predators. Did she dive for leftovers from a white shark's seal meal? Or follow schools of hunting bluefin?

Sooty shearwaters spend 90 percent of their lives at sea.

By the end of September, fall comes to Japan. Something tells the male shearwater it is time to return to New Zealand. Perhaps it is the cooler weather or the shortening of the daylight. The male catches winds now blowing south. FLAP-FLAP-FLAP-*g l i d e*. FLAP-FLAP-FLAP-*g l i d e*. He is back on Codfish Island just ten days after leaving Japan. His mate takes a little longer—three weeks—to get from California to New Zealand.

During their ten-month trip, the sooty shearwaters visit some of the richest waters in the entire Pacific Ocean. They power their journey with the gift of the wind and their own steady hearts.

On October 16 the pair meets again on Codfish Island. After long days aloft, with only the sound of the wind and the waves, it must be jarring to hear the noisy moaning of thousands of seabirds. But snuggling back in burrow #B111, neither seems to mind.

Shearwater pairs spend a lot of time side by side. They groom each other with their bills and stare at each other like teenagers in love.

Why do sooty shearwaters travel so far? Good feeding areas are far apart. The birds' figure-eight route uses steady winds to propel them to the Pacific's best dining areas. Over ten months, the male traveled 58,700 miles (94,470 kilometers). The female traveled 44,440 miles (71,520 kilometers). On an average day, each flew more than 200 miles (320 kilometers).

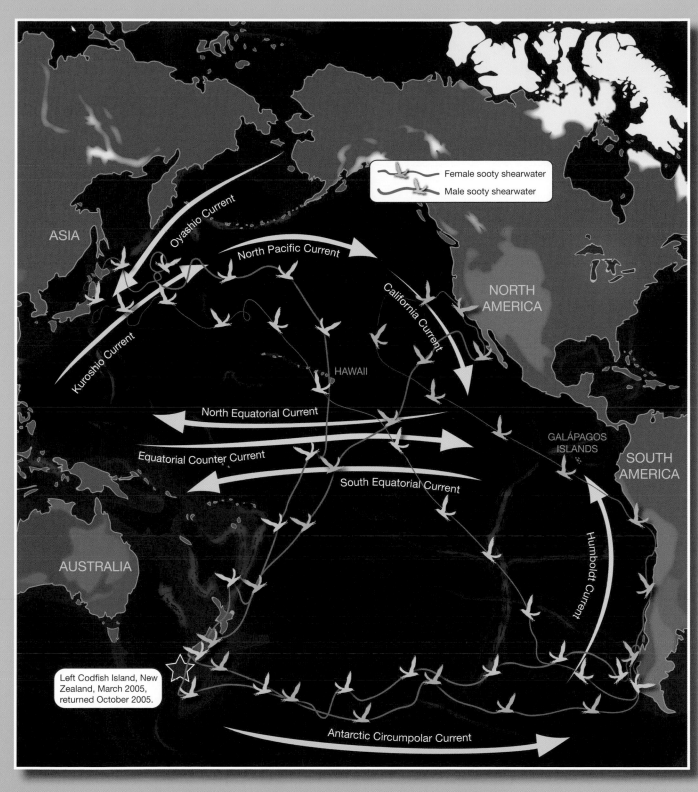

Female sooty shearwater
Male sooty shearwater

ASIA

Oyashio Current

North Pacific Current

California Current

NORTH AMERICA

Kuroshio Current

HAWAII

North Equatorial Current

Equatorial Counter Current

GALÁPAGOS ISLANDS

SOUTH AMERICA

South Equatorial Current

AUSTRALIA

Humboldt Current

Left Codfish Island, New Zealand, March 2005, returned October 2005.

Antarctic Circumpolar Current

CONCLUSION
Lessons from the Blue

Scientists have learned a great deal by using high-tech tags on ocean predators. Leatherbacks that nest in Costa Rica follow a predictable route past the Galápagos Islands. Bluefin tuna don't just cross the Pacific once or twice; they may cross it many times. White sharks don't just swim along the coast; they journey far offshore—sometimes all the way to Hawaii. Sooty shearwaters don't fly in a big circle around the Pacific; they travel in a giant figure eight. As TOPP scientist Andre Boustany says: "I've seen enough incredible behavior and migrations from these animals that a fish would have to travel on land to really amaze me."

Sea turtles have been swimming in our oceans since the time of the dinosaurs. But they won't survive much longer without our protection.

The tag research can help the animals too. Scientists and conservationists are trying to find a way to protect wildlife living in the open oceans from overfishing and other threats. One idea is to create ocean parks. On land we don't allow hunting everywhere. National parks protect animals like bears, wolves, and elk. Why not protect our ocean wildlife the same way?

The tags show that some parts of the ocean, like the California Current, the Humboldt Current, and the seamounts east of Japan, are very important to Pacific predators. The predators visit these rich fishing grounds to find food and mates.

These areas are important to fishermen too. But if some parts of these feeding grounds are protected, our ocean wildlife will have safe places to live and grow. We may not always see or hear them, but they will be out there, prowling the seas.

Shearwaters dive to capture fish, shrimp, and squid. The deepest dive made by the tagged female shearwater was 131 feet (40 meters). The male dived to 164 feet (50 meters).

A tagged yellowfin tuna is released by TOPP scientists. Turn to the Resources section on page 39 to learn more about how you can follow TOPP animals online.

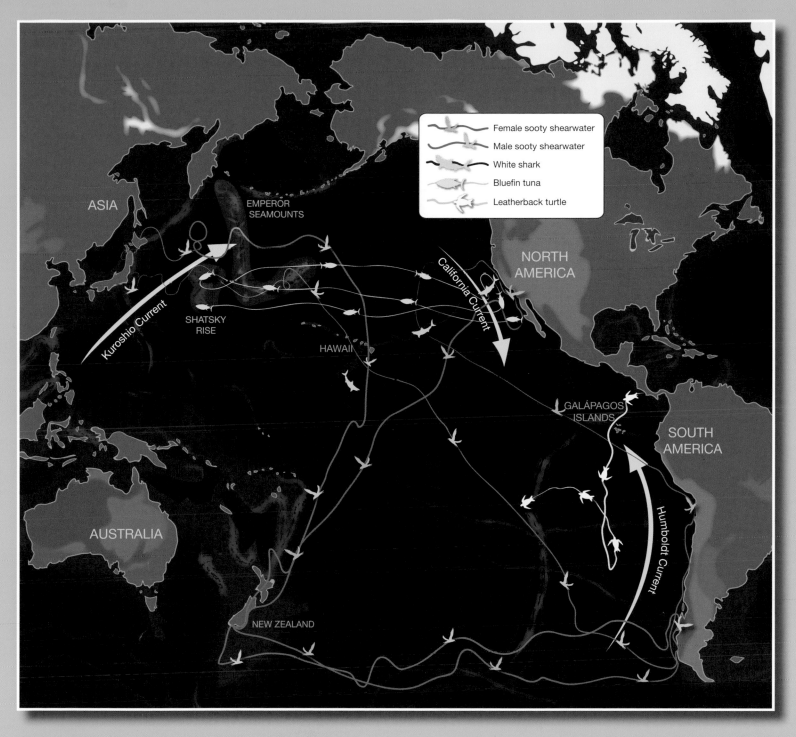

Ocean predators find good eating along coastal currents
and around islands and underwater mountains.

OCEAN PREDATOR POPULATIONS

Leatherback Sea Turtle

In 1982 there were an estimated 115,000 female leatherbacks worldwide (since females must come out of the water to lay their eggs, they are easier to count than males). By 1996 the number of females had fallen to 34,500. The decline in leatherbacks nesting on Playa Grande in Costa Rica was even more drastic. The number of nesting females fell from about 1,000 in 1990 to about 100 in 2005—a 90 percent decline.

Bluefin Tuna

Scientists often use fishery data to help them track fish populations. They measure how many tons of the fish are being caught, compared to the catch in previous years. Scientists adjust these numbers according to the effort required to catch the fish (for example, the number of hooks in the water). These data suggest that 90 percent of all large predatory fish (tuna, marlin, swordfish, sharks, cod, and halibut) are gone. Bluefin, the most valuable fish in the sea, are hardest hit by overfishing.

White Shark

White sharks are found in many parts of the world, most notably off the coasts of California, Australia, and South Africa. No one knows how many there are, but as a top predator their numbers are probably low. The California Department of Fish and Game estimates there may be fewer than 100 adult white sharks along the entire California coast.

Sooty Shearwater

There are an estimated 20 million sooty shearwaters worldwide. However, 1–12 million birds have been killed by driftnet fisheries in the last fifty years. Scientists have recently documented declines of 30 percent or more in some locations.

RESOURCES

For Further Reading

Lasky, Kathryn. *Interrupted Journey: Saving Endangered Sea Turtles.* Cambridge: Candlewick Press, 2001.

Markle, Sandra. *Outside and Inside Sharks.* New York: Atheneum, 1996.

Ryder, Joanne. *Shark in the Sea.* New York: Morrow Junior Books, 1997.

Webb, Sophie. *Looking for Seabirds: Journal from an Alaskan Voyage.* Boston: Houghton Mifflin, 2004.

Internet Resources

Tagging of Pacific Predators: http://www.topp.org

The Great Turtle Race: http://www.greatturtlerace.com

Multimedia

The Blue Planet, DVD. Directed by Alastair Fothergill. Glasgow: BBC Video, 2002.

"Ocean Deep" and "Shallow Seas." *Planet Earth*, DVD. Directed by Alastair Fothergill. Glasgow: BBC Video, 2007.

Of Special Interest to Educators

Ocean-focused lesson plans and resources from National Geographic:

> http://www.nationalgeographic.com/seas

. . . and Monterey Bay Aquarium:

> http://www.mbayaq.org/lc/teachers_place/resources.asp

Google Ocean now includes a special animal-tracking layer, the Global Tagging of Pelagic Predators, that uses fly-through animations to provide an animal's-eye-view of the underwater world. Tag along with tuna, sharks, whales, seals, sea turtles, and seabirds at http://earth.google.com and http://www.gtopp.org.

What You Can Do

Read this comprehensive, thoughtful list from the Smithsonian National Museum of Natural History:

> http://www.ocean.si.edu/ocean_hall/what_you_can_do.html

For Jacob and Coleen

First published in the United States of America in 2009 by Walker Publishing Company, Inc.
Visit Walker & Company's Web site at www.walkeryoungreaders.com

For information about permission to reproduce selections from this book, write to
Permissions, Walker & Company, 175 Fifth Avenue, New York, New York 10010

Library of Congress Cataloging-in-Publication Data
Turner, Pamela S.
Prowling the seas : exploring the hidden world of ocean predators / Pamela S. Turner.
p.   cm.
ISBN-13: 978-0-8027-9748-3 • ISBN-10: 0-8027-9748-2 (hardcover)
ISBN-13: 978-0-8027-9749-0 • ISBN-10: 0-8027-9749-0 (reinforced)
1. Predatory marine animals—Juvenile literature. I. Title.
QL122.2.T88 2009   591.5'309162—dc22   2009008375

Typeset in Weidemann
Book design by Nicole Gastonguay

Printed in China by SNP Leefung Printers Limited
(hardcover) 10 9 8 7 6 5 4 3 2 1
(reinforced) 10 9 8 7 6 5 4 3 2 1

ACKNOWLEDGMENTS

My deepest thanks to the TOPP scientists: Barbara Block, Scot Anderson, Andre Boustany, George Shillinger, and Scott Shaffer, who answered endless questions and took time from their busy lives to review and comment on this manuscript. I am also indebted to Scot Anderson, Barbara Block, Christian Bonham, Andre Boustany, Jason Bradley, Sam McKechnie, Monterey Bay Aquarium, Kasia Newman, Jeff Poklen, Darren Scott, Scott Shaffer, and Franz and Calvin Wisner for the wonderful photos. To Valerie Krist, thank you for creating pitch-perfect graphics. Nicole Gastonguay contributed a stunning book design.

I am particularly grateful to my editor, Emily Easton, for letting me include bluefin—the underrated, overfished Porsche of the sea.

PHOTO CREDITS

Scot Anderson—6 (salmon shark), 22, 23, 24, 26
Chuck Babbitt/iStockphoto.com—6 (albatross)
Franco Banfi/SeaPics.com—6 (squid)
Barbara Block—14, 16 (left)
Christian Bonham—25, 38 (shark)
Andre Boustany—36
Jason Bradley—cover (shark/turtles), 4, 8, 9, 10, 11, 12, 21, 38 (turtle)
Ryan Burke/iStockphoto.com—graphic: 3
Chris & Monique Fallows/OceanwideImages.com—35
Jamie Farrant/iStockphoto.com—graphic: 5, 8, 14, 20, 28, 34
David T. Gomez/iStockphoto.com—6 (sea lion)
Richard Hermann/SeaPics.com—18 (left), 38 (tuna)
Michel Jozon/SeaPics.com—6 (sperm whale)
Valerie Krist—back cover illustrations, folio icons, graphic: 13, 17, 19, 27, 33, 37
Sam McKechnie—29
Monterey Bay Aquarium/Randy Wilder—cover (tuna), 6 (tuna and sunfish), 15, 16 (right)
Doug Perrine/SeaPics.com—34
Jeff Poklen—cover (seabird), 30, 31, 38 (shearwater)
Darren Scott—6 (shearwater), 32
Scott Shaffer—28 (top and bottom)
Elizabeth Tighe-Andino/iStockphoto.com—1
Pamela S. Turner—6 (elephant seal), 18 (right)
Doc White/SeaPics.com—2–3
Joseph White/iStockphoto.com—6 (turtle)
Franz Wisner—20